WORKING *as a* TEACHER *in* YOUR COMMUNITY

Sophia Natasha Sunseri

ROSEN
PUBLISHING®

New York

Published in 2016 by The Rosen Publishing Group, Inc.
29 East 21st Street, New York, NY 10010

Library of Congress Cataloging-in-Publication Data

Sunseri, Sophia Natasha.
Working as a teacher in your community/Sophia Natasha Sunseri.
    pages cm.—(Careers in your community)
Includes bibliographical references and index.
ISBN 978-1-4994-6117-6 (library bound)
1. Teachers—Juvenile literature. 2. Teaching—Vocational guidance—
Juvenile literature. I. Title.
LB1775.S865 2016
371.102—dc23

                                        2014045478

Manufactured in the United States of America

Contents

Introduction

Schools are at the very heart of our society. Schools are where we learn. They're where we become well versed in math, English, history, and other fundamental subjects. Schools are where we first socialize and learn to treat others with respect. They are where we learn to discover our individuality and where we learn the value of teamwork and fellowship. At their core, schools are where we learn how to learn. And if schools are at the heart of society, teachers are the blood that keeps the heart beating.

One of the main reasons that many educators enter the teaching profession is because they want to have meaningful impacts on their communities and on the world at large. Teachers play unique and formative roles in their students' lives by providing them with the critical thinking tools necessary to become successful and productive members of the communities in which they live. Rebecca K., a certified English teacher who instructs students in grades 6–12, puts it succinctly: "I want to help my students become active and dynamic participants in society." When teachers invest in their students by giving them the tools they need to become active participants in society, they are also investing in their students' families and in the well-being of their communities.

Teaching is a profession where the fruits of your labor go beyond the individual person.

As a teacher, you will have the opportunity to be a positive influence in your students' lives and in your community at large.

Teaching empowers an educator not only to impart knowledge to his or her students but also to prepare young people to become responsible, upstanding citizens who are driven by strong values and strong minds—fueled with a sense of wonder and a desire to dream big. Just by going to work every day, teachers can realize the opportunity of making a deep and lasting impact on the future of our world. If you want to make an impact on your community and feel a deep sense of pride in your career, then you may just be on your way to a career in teaching.

Here we will discuss the ins and outs of teaching: what the job entails, the requirements needed to become a teacher, the career opportunities that are available for those interested in the teaching profession, ways to land an interview, and the exciting future that awaits you once you become a teacher.

CHAPTER One

What Does a Career in Teaching Involve?

For somebody interested in teaching, there are plenty of opportunities available. Before taking the steps toward a career in education, it's important to first understand the basics of the job and consider the kind of position that may interest you. One question you may want to ask is how many hours you would like to work each week. Depending on the answer, you might consider a position as a substitute teacher, as a teaching assistant, or as a full-time teacher—each of which has varying job requirements and schedules. Some other things to consider are the age group that you are most interested in teaching or whether you would feel more comfortable teaching at a public school or in a private school.

By thinking about the basic questions mentioned above, somebody who is interested in a teaching career can explore all the possibilities that such a career has to offer. While these choices sound exciting, they can also be overwhelming. Later we will discuss how to narrow them down, but regardless of the position chosen, there are some general qualities that apply to almost all teaching jobs. Learning about these characteristics will give somebody intrigued by teaching the first sign of whether or not this career might be the right fit!

General Duties

Teachers are expected to wear many hats. First and foremost, teachers are responsible for imparting knowledge. This means that teachers should possess excellent written and oral communication skills so that they can relay information in a clear and engaging manner. Within this role, teachers' general duties include sharing and explaining new information and skills in the classroom, assigning and evaluating homework assignments, and analyzing students' progress (thereby ensuring that students are performing at grade level and are prepared to meet testing standards). In order to accomplish these goals, the ideal teacher is a highly organized person and works well in group settings. He or she must demonstrate the ability to thoughtfully interact with students, parents, other teachers, and school administrators.

Teachers should be prepared to assume other roles as well. In addition to acting as instructors, teachers are also expected to act as:

- *Mentors Students look up to teachers and rely on them for guidance in decisions related to their education as well as their social life. Therefore, it is of vital importance that a teacher be aware of his or her behavior and the example that he or she is setting at all times.*

Solving Simple Equations Sec. 3.1 - 3.3

$$x - 7 = -21$$

$$x - (-15) = 2$$

$$\frac{3}{5}y = 9$$

A teacher's primary task is to relay information in an effective manner while captivating students' attention and interest.

- *Counselors* If a student experiences an emotional or behavioral issue, a teacher will be expected to recognize the situation and contact the school counselor or the student's parents.

- *Disciplinarians* If a student is being disruptive, a teacher should be adept at addressing the problem in an assertive but fair manner. Teachers need to be confident in handling these situations appropriately.

Work Schedule

The majority of full-time elementary school, middle school, and high school teachers work more than the standard forty hours a week that most full-time adult employees work. This is because in addition to the duties that they perform inside the classroom, teachers must also prepare outside classroom hours. Teachers often write lesson plans and grade assignments outside school hours or during their time at home. Often, preschool teachers, substitute teachers, and teaching assistants are exceptions to this rule. These teachers either have fewer obligations in terms of lesson planning and homework assignments or work only part-time.

Most full-time teachers work ten months out of the year and enjoy a two-month paid summer vacation. While some teachers choose to relax during their summer vacation, others teach summer school, have temporary part-time jobs, or pursue continuing education (meaning additional college degrees or certifications of their own). Preschool teachers are once again an exception, usually working year-round.

Most students agree that teachers play instrumental roles in their lives.

Salary and Benefits

The salary of a teacher can vary, largely depending on the kind of position a teacher has (as a substitute teacher, a teaching assistant, or a full-time teacher) as well as on the state in which he or she works. A teacher's salary can also be affected by the type of secondary education, degrees, or certifications that the teacher has and the length of time for which he or she has been employed. For example, in most states a teacher who holds a master's degree in teaching or education will generally earn more than a teacher who holds just a bachelor's degree. An ESL (English as a second language)–certified teacher might receive a higher salary than a teacher who does not have the same certification to teach students whose first languages are something other than English. For current information about teacher salaries in your state, please refer to the Bureau of Labor and Statistics website: www.bls.gov.

In addition to the salary, somebody interested in teaching should keep in mind that many teaching positions come with attractive benefits packages. Benefits are extras given to employees by an employer beyond the employee's basic salary. Not all benefits packages are the same, but many teachers get benefits that include: contributions to the state retirement system, paid sick leave, health insurance, and dental insurance Other contracts might include long-term disability insurance, emergency leave, and financial investment options. A career in teaching can help ensure a stable financial future and great retirement options when the time arrives.

SPOTLIGHT ON TEACHERS WHO INSPIRE: DR. LISA DELPIT

Dr. Lisa Delpit is a Harvard University–educated professor best known for her work in the urban school system. Deemed "one of the most important writers in education today" in a March 1996 article in *Education Week*, Delpit values students' cultural strengths, and she champions diversity in the classroom. In her book *Other People's Children: Cultural Conflict in the Classroom*, Delpit explains that not all children have the same needs and that teaching methods that work for one student population may not work for all groups of students. In particular, Delpit questions popular teaching methods aimed at African American students. "Teaching is like telling a story," Delpit says. "But you have to look at people while you're telling the story and you can't tell the same story to everyone."

Delpit has made many contributions to the field of education, both inside and outside the classroom. As a college professor, Delpit has taught classes such as Readings in Urban Excellence, where she exposed students at Georgia State University to the writings of urban educators including Herbert Kohl, Vivian Gussin Paley, and Gloria Ladson-Billings. In the 1980s, she published a number of influential essays in the *Harvard Educational Review*, perhaps the most notable being "Skills and Other Dilemmas of a Progressive Black Educator." Through these essays, Delpit helped educators better understand issues surrounding racial insensitivity in schools. Furthermore, in 1996 Delpit helped launch the Atlanta-based Alonzo A. Crim Center on Urban Education Excellence, which works

(continued on the next page)

At Georgia State University and elsewhere, Dr. Lisa Delpit has praised the writings of urban educators and promoted diversity in the classroom.

(*continued from the previous page*)

with educators in that city's school system on school-improvement projects.

Delpit has earned numerous accolades for her work, including a MacArthur Genius Grant (1990), an Outstanding Contribution to Education: Harvard Graduate School of Education Award (1993), an American Education Research Association Cattell Award for Outstanding Career Achievement (1994), and the Antioch College Horace Mann Humanity Award (2003). Her teachings serve as a crucial reminder that communities are often comprised of diverse populations and that educators who are hoping to enrich their respective communities must bear this diversity in mind, acknowledge diversity in the classroom, and create nuanced lesson plans that cater to different student populations.

The Rewards of Being a Teacher

As with any job, a career in teaching can be both rewarding and challenging. Let's look at some of the many benefits that a career in teaching has to offer. First, many educators agree that the opportunity to make a difference in their communities is one of the major perks of teaching. Teachers inspire students and give them the tools they need to grow, ultimately having a lasting impact on their futures. A successful career in teaching can be very personally fulfilling. As Nora C., an early childhood education graduate student at Bank Street College in New York, New York, confirms, "Watching a child take pride in him- or herself as he or she gains skills, learns to problem solve, and become passionate about learning is priceless."

A career in teaching is also a career that you can count on. There will always be a need for teachers. In addition to knowing that you are helping to enrich your community, you can also have a greater degree of job security in a rapidly changing world. Even as technological developments change the classroom, educators still play an integral role in guiding students and overseeing collective learning. Furthermore, teachers get ten enviable weeks of paid summer vacation. Most corporate jobs offer only between two and four weeks of paid vacation. This, of course, is not the primary reason why somebody should consider a career in teaching, but it is a nice perk.

A Challenging Job, Too

Along with the many satisfying aspects of being a teacher come a handful of more challenging ones.

A career in teaching comes with challenges and can require a great deal of patience and skilled classroom management.

Many teachers describe their job as having high stress factors. A teacher sometimes may have to manage a classroom full of rambunctious students or effectively handle the behavioral and disciplinary issues that will inevitably arise. Kristin Ann F., a certified teacher of grades 9–12 on Long Island, New York, expounds upon some of the challenges she faced: "Like many new teachers, my main challenge was classroom management. I was very close in age to my students when I first began teaching, so setting strict boundaries was crucial to my success—as well as theirs! . . . I wasn't there to be my students' cool, young teacher-friend, I was there to be their mentor, and without learning to assert myself I believe my career would have suffered as would my students' education."

Beyond the difficulties of managing large groups of students, teachers face the added pressures of having to administer standardized tests, many of which are results-driven and are often used to measure a teacher's success. Teachers are also required to work long hours. Teachers must often arrive at school before classes start to set up for the day and will oftentimes stay after classes are out to clean up or grade assignments. Assignments to grade and lessons to plan often follow teachers home in the evenings or on weekends.

While it is important to be aware of these challenges that teachers face, it is also important not to be too daunted by them. Instead, be aware that these difficulties exist and be proactive about developing methods to help you manage them. At the end of the day, most teachers agree that the rewards of teaching far outweigh the challenges. Brian L., a dean at a Queens, New York, middle school elaborates: "If a person is considering teaching as their chosen profession for the security, benefits, and vacations, then they are not entering for the right reasons… If a person is truly entering the profession of teaching to help students grow academically, emotionally, and socially, then it can be one of the most rewarding experiences in a person's life." If you're intrigued by the idea of making an impact as a teacher, it may just be the right career for you!

CHAPTER Two

Building Skills: The Right Training and Education

There are specific character traits that are especially conducive to becoming a good teacher. Included among them are patience, flexibility, creative problem-solving abilities, excellent organizational and communication skills, and being able to manage stressful situations. Another useful skill for teachers is to feel comfortable in front of large groups of people. While many people might not necessarily think of it this way, teachers must often act as though they are performers. They must think about such things as projecting their voice and using engaging body language. Think of some of your own favorite teachers and the ways in which they held your attention or kept class interesting.

In addition to these basic character traits that make for an engaging instructor, all teachers must go through some form of training and certification before they can begin in the classroom. Depending on the position sought, this process will be different, but some general steps are common to all teaching jobs.

Training and Practical Experience

One of the best ways to figure out early if a teaching career is right for you is to try it. There are many teaching opportunities—in the forms of internships and volunteer positions—that do not require a certificate or degree in education. In addition to providing valuable teaching experience, these opportunities are also wonderful ways for somebody to contribute to his or her community at an early age. There are quite a few organizations that somebody in high school or college can check out.

One great program is the America Reads Challenge. The America Reads Challenge was started in 1996 by former president Bill Clinton's administration with the aim of improving national literacy. The campaign depends on "volunteer tutors ready and able to give children the personal attention they need to catch up and get ahead." The American Reads Challenge is looking for tutors who can help teach students from kindergarten through sixth grade how to read.

Teach for America, meanwhile, provides poverty-stricken children with quality educations. Corps members typically come from diverse backgrounds. While some have a background in education, many others do not have any previous teaching experience. Teach for America looks for future teachers who have leadership potential. According to the organization's website: "Your potential as a corps member can shine through whether you've led your student government, managed a complex project at work, achieved academic honors, served our country in the armed forces, or rallied support for a cause that's important to

SPOTLIGHT ON TEACHERS WHO INSPIRE: BOOKER T. WASHINGTON

Booker T. Washington (1856–1915) is the most influential black educator of his time. He is accredited with almost single-handedly controlling the money allocated to black schools and colleges during the late nineteenth century.

Born a slave on a farm in Virginia, Washington overcame incredible odds during his lifetime. Determined to receive an education, he traveled hundreds of miles to Hampton University—a historically black college established in 1868—where he pursued industrial education. Education and industry, Washington believed, were paths through which African Americans could attain self-reliance and, ultimately, equality. After his time at Hampton University, his successes continued to

Booker T. Washington is an example of how teaching can be a viable way to effect change in your community and in the world at large.

flourish. In 1881, Washington founded the Tuskegee Institute, a black school in Alabama for training teachers. Shortly thereafter, in 1901, he helped form the National Negro Business League. Washington also served as an adviser to presidents Theodore Roosevelt and William Howard Taft. His acclaimed autobiography, *Up from Slavery* (1901), is still widely read and is considered a classic in the genre of narratives by American self-made men.

Full-Time Teaching Positions

Somebody interested in becoming an elementary, middle, or secondary school teacher must first earn a bachelor's degree. In many states, this degree must be specifically in education and must be granted by an approved teacher-education program. In addition, teachers-to-be must become licensed in their state. Each of the fifty states has different specific requirements, though most mandate the completion of a teacher education program, such as a bachelor's degree program in education, and the passage of a state-administered exam. Many also require supervised teaching experience. Once licensed, teachers may have to participate in periodic testing or continuing education courses in order to keep their license up to date so they may continue teaching.

Elementary school teachers have slightly different requirements than middle school or high school teachers. They often must enroll in elementary or early childhood education degree programs that focus on foundations of education and educational psychology. They must also demonstrate sufficient knowledge of the various subjects taught at elementary school grade level.

Substitute Teachers

Requirements for substitute teachers vary by employer and by state. While some schools and states require a bachelor's degree and a state teaching certification, others require only a high school diploma or a GED.

Teaching Assistants

Many school districts and federal programs require that teacher's aides have at least two years of college or an associate's degree. Prospective students interested in becoming teacher's aides should look into Associate of Applied Science (AAS) programs, most of which allow students to work in classrooms under the supervision of a licensed teacher.

Which Position Is Right for Me?

As mentioned earlier, teaching assistant and substitute teacher positions can be viable—and highly desirable—employment options for people seeking part-time work or more flexible schedules. However, it is important to bear in mind that obtaining a bachelor's degree in education and seeking full-time employment as a teacher has its advantages.

According to the U.S. Census Bureau, college graduates earn an average of 80 percent more income than people without college degrees (while people with master's degrees earn a whopping 170 percent more!). They also tend to enjoy a higher standard of living and have a more robust sense of accomplishment and fulfillment. Obtaining the necessary prerequisites to acquire your teacher's license will inevitably ensure greater job security and a more stable future. The world will always need dedicated teachers to help enrich its respective communities.

Financing Your Education

While a college education can significantly advance the career opportunities available to a young person interested in teaching, costs are an important consideration. Many students may consider applying

There are many options available to students looking to finance their education, including student loans, scholarships, and grants.

to schools that are located in the state where they live because state schools are significantly less expensive than out-of-state schools. If you choose to attend a school out of state, you will have to think wisely about financing your education.

As you begin thinking about how to finance your education, consider applying for financial aid. Most universities in the United States and Canada offer financial aid options to students. In the United States, these funds are available through the United States Department of Education, which provides loans at low interest rates to students. The students are then expected to begin paying these loans back after graduation. Federal aid can be used to pay for expenses such as tuition and fees, room and board, books and supplies, and transportation.

After being accepted to a college or university, a prospective student can file for financial aid for free by filling out an application at the Free Application for Federal Student Aid (FAFSA) website: https://fafsa .ed.gov. After doing so, students will automatically be considered for federal, state, and college financial assistance programs. A college counselor or a high school guidance counselor is the best resource for any questions a student may have about the financial aid application process. A counselor will help a student sift through the paperwork and guide him or her in the right direction.

Student Loan Forgiveness Programs

Another thing for prospective college students interested in teaching to bear in mind is that there are two types of student loan forgiveness programs

TYPES OF FINANCIAL AID

There are several different kinds of financial aid available for students in the United States. Depending on your finances, your academic background, and the colleges to which you are accepted, a financial aid package may consist of a combination of different types of financial aid. The common categories of financial aid include:

- *Need-based grants, including Federal Pell Grants and Federal Supplemental Education Opportunity Grants (SEOG), are grants awarded to students by the federal government based on a student's financial need.*

- *Need-based student loans, including Federal Direct Subsidized Stafford loans and Federal Perkins loans, are loans given by the federal government to students who cannot afford the cost of college. They must be repaid.*

- *Non-need-based student loans, such as Federal Direct Unsubsidized loans, are loans that are available to students regardless of financial need.*

- *Federal direct PLUS loans are loans offered by the U.S. Department of Education aimed at graduate students and the parents of dependent undergraduate students to help pay for college or career school.*

Requirements vary in determining eligibility for different types of financial assistance, so research carefully before determining what package is best fit to your finances and needs.

for teachers. The first, the Teacher Loan Forgiveness Program, is intended to foster a passion for teaching. Under this program, teachers who work full-time for five consecutive academic years at specific elementary and secondary schools and educational service agencies in low-income school districts may qualify for loan forgiveness of up to $17,500 on direct subsidized and unsubsidized loans as well as on subsidized and unsubsidized federal Stafford loans. (A student who has only PLUS loans, however, is ineligible.)

The second such program is the Teacher Cancellation Program. Under this program, recipients who hold federal Perkins loans may qualify for loan cancellation if they choose to teach full-time at a low-income school or in certain subject areas.

For more information on student loan forgiveness programs for teachers, please consult the Federal Student Aid website: https://studentaid.ed.gov.

Searching for Scholarships

Another option that every student should consider is applying for scholarships or grants—money that doesn't ever have to be paid back. Many universities offer their own scholarships or grants as a part of their financial aid package. Students can contact the schools to which they are applying in order to learn more about additional funding opportunities.

There are also outside sources of scholarship and grant funding. A student doesn't need to have perfect grades or be one of the top students in his or her class in order to qualify for certain scholarships. There are lots of different scholarships and grants available to students from different academic, ethnic, and socioeconomic backgrounds. Before beginning the search, however, remember that legitimate scholarship and financial aid should always be free; you should never have to pay for financial aid assistance.

With a combination of loans, grants, and scholarships, paying for a degree in education shouldn't be a burden. And once you're armed with the right education and certifications, the job hunt for a career in teaching can begin!

CHAPTER Three

Kick-Starting Your Career

We've already discussed several ways in which you can acquire teaching experience and give back to your community in the process, including internships and volunteer opportunities. Hopefully, these experiences will have given you an idea of which age groups and what subjects you prefer to teach. After determining that teaching is the right career for you and completing the necessary educational and certification requirements, it is time to start thinking about the best ways to go about looking for work as a teacher.

Preparing for the Job Hunt

After completing your educational and certification requirements, including any college education you've pursued and state teaching certification exams you've taken, you may be thinking, "Now what?" Before a job candidate sends out a résumé to potential employers, a smart first step is to make sure that his or her portfolio is in order. Since recent college graduates are likely to have limited teaching experience, it is of the utmost importance that they impress their potential employers and stand out in other ways.

Before embarking on the job hunt, every candidate should make sure that the contents of his or her teaching portfolio are in order.

One way to stand out is with a teaching portfolio. A teaching portfolio should include materials that show that you are a strong candidate, including transcripts, proof of certification, letters of recommendation, a statement of teaching philosophy, sample lesson plans, and work from student teaching. A trusted friend who is already a teacher or a college professor might be willing to proofread the contents of your portfolio and suggest improvements. Remember that these documents are a professional representation of a job candidate. A portfolio marred with typos and grammatical errors will make an employer think twice about a candidate's ability to communicate effectively.

How to Structure a Teaching Philosophy Statement

A teaching philosophy statement should reflect two things about a teaching candidate: the candidate's personal values and how he or she will meet the educational needs of students. Lee Haugen of Iowa State University's Center for Excellence in Teaching and Learning (CETL) suggests organizing a teaching philosophy statement in four sections:

To What End?

This section should list a candidate's objectives as a teacher. Start by stating your end point, or what you hope your students will gain in the long run. Beyond learning the basic content of the course, what do you hope students will achieve? Could it be lifelong critical-thinking skills? Problem-solving strategies? Specify how you will facilitate these objectives.

By What Means?

After establishing teaching objectives, a teaching philosophy statement should discuss how you plan to implement them. What methods will be employed? This is your chance to show off knowledge of learning theory, cognitive development, and curriculum design. This is the spot to explain, for example, how to go about choosing syllabus readings or whether you would opt to assign group projects or individual projects. The methodology should always relate back to the objectives listed in the previous section.

To What Degree?

This is the section in which you can discuss how you will measure the effectiveness of your teaching. Assessing student outcomes is one viable way of doing so. If, for example, one objective is to foster problem-solving strategies, you may want to begin by testing your students' ability to solve problems. Then, this section can discuss your thought process: how you would decide what problems to give students to solve, how you would construct those problems, what skills those problems are meant to evaluate, and the level of performance that you are seeking.

Why?

In this final section, a candidate can get creative. Here, you can discuss the rewards of teaching. How does teaching improve your community or make the world a better place? From where do you derive your interest in this career over any other? Answering questions such as these just might give you the favorable edge over competition.

After having built—and thoroughly proofread—a portfolio, job seekers can start looking for teaching jobs in their area. Don't wait for employers to contact you. Be proactive. Make a job-hunting schedule and stick to it every day. Having a to-do list where you jot down the goals you hope to accomplish can be a useful strategy for keeping busy while on the hunt for a job.

Reach Out

Network, network, network! Reach out to friends, colleagues, classmates, and school administrators.

You never know when someone will hear about a job for which you'd be a great fit. Also be sure to take advantage of social media. Spread the word on websites such as Facebook and network on LinkedIn, a career-specific social media website. The job search website CareerBuilder has several regional Twitter feeds where candidates might find job postings in their area.

In addition to networking among acquaintances and online, job seekers can consult career resource centers at their school, attend career fairs, and scan local newspapers for job openings. There are also free teacher placement services, such as Want to Teach and Teachers-Teachers. These popular placement services are used by school districts to fill vacancies

Networking among family, friends, and colleagues may help you land your dream job. Career fairs are also great places to network.

and are a great place to check for new job openings. Many education jobs are also posted on the National Education Association (NEA) state affiliates job board. By visiting its website and clicking on a specific state, job seekers can view the various teaching jobs available in their area.

The National Education Association (NEA) is an organization committed to protecting and advancing the interests of educators in the United States. Pictured here are its headquarters.

A specific organization that is always looking to recruit teachers is EnCorps. The EnCorps Teachers Program recruits teachers and tutors with backgrounds in science, technology, engineering, and math (STEM) areas of knowledge to work with children in disadvantaged communities. The program aims to close the achievement gap by equipping its students with the knowledge they will need to become leaders in the aforementioned industries. The websites and contact information for these organizations and similar ones are included in the For More Information section at the end of this resource.

SPOTLIGHT ON TEACHERS WHO INSPIRE: EMMA WILLARD

Emma Willard (1787–1870) was a leading innovator in education for women. In 1814, she founded the first higher education institution for women in the United States, the Middlebury Female Seminary, which was based out of her Vermont home. Willard helped pave the way for young women interested in studying math, science, and the classics, proving that her female students could master these subjects just as well as their male counterparts. The Middlebury Female Seminary was a precursor to the Emma Willard School, an all-girls boarding school that Willard later opened in Troy, New York. The Emma Willard School continues in operation to this day as a college preparatory school. In the 1960s, the Troy campus was declared a National Historic Landmark.

In addition to being renowned for having founded the Middlebury Female Seminary and the Emma Willard School, Willard is also highly regarded for her

The Emma Willard School is a National Historic Landmark, commemorating Willard's career as well as the advancements that have been made in girls' and women's education.

Plan for Improving Female Education (1918)—the first proposal of its kind to mandate publicly funded schools for girls. The plan is considered a pivotal document in the history of women's education in the United States. Though portions of Willard's proposal would be considered dated by today's standards, its influence is still widespread. Willard's efforts as an educator resulted in the offering of advanced studies to girls, enabling an increasing number of women to play more central roles in their communities.

Follow the Demand

If you experience difficulty finding teaching jobs where you live, think about alternative ways to make yourself marketable. For example, a candidate can significantly improve the chances of finding work if he or she has dual certification, for instance if somebody is certified to teach both English and math. There may not be a need for English teachers in an area, but there may be a higher demand for math teachers. The National Education Association Academy offers free or discounted courses for professional development (and in some cases for graduate credit) that can be applied toward dual certification.

If a candidate is willing to relocate, he or she may also significantly improve the chances of finding work as a teacher. A little research can reveal what regions are hiring and have a greater demand for teachers. The U.S. Department of Education issues an annual report entitled "Teacher Shortage Areas Nationwide Listing," which is a great resource for detailed information about geographic and subject area shortages for each state. The report furthermore documents how teacher shortages in specific regions or subject areas have fluctuated since 1990. Some parts of the country that are in need of teachers offer attractive incentive packages, too. Some have robust recruitment programs or offer relocation services.

Bon Voyage: Teaching Abroad

Pursuing a teaching job abroad can be an excellent way to travel, be exposed to different cultures, gain valuable teaching experience, and save money.

Teaching abroad can give you the opportunity to travel the world and learn about communities other than your own.

Typically, programs that sponsor English teachers cover airfare, housing, transportation, and daily living expenses for the duration of the teaching contract. Don't worry—candidates don't need to be fluent in any language other than English. While most programs do not require a background in education or teaching, they usually stipulate that teachers be native English speakers and that they hold at least a bachelor's degree (in any field). Contracts often range from six months to two years (sometimes with an option to renew).

There are a wealth of online resources for scouting out international teaching jobs and learning more about what they entail. Popular teaching destinations range across continents. These can be a great opportunity for somebody seeking to build up teaching experience and travel to a new and exciting destination.

CHAPTER Four

Nailing the Job Interview

You've landed a job interview for a teaching position. Congratulations! Your hard work has paid off. Now that you have your foot in the door, it is time to start thinking about how you will nail the interview. In order to make the interview successful, you will need to prepare for it. Basic interviewing tips and etiquette are the keys to a successful interview.

How to Dress for Success

The first impression that a candidate makes on a potential employer is of the utmost importance. A person's physical appearance is arguably as significant as credentials and how he or she performs during the actual interview. According to Frank Bernieri, Ph.D., associate professor of psychology at Oregon State University, an interviewer will determine whether or not somebody is a good fit for the position within the first ten seconds of meeting the person. A candidate who is neat and professional in appearance is therefore more likely to be hired than one who is unkempt and disheveled. Bernieri cautions that dressing the

Being appropriately attired is crucial to making a good impression during a job interview.

wrong way for an interview is comparable to "picking your nose in public." This does not mean that you need to go out and spend lots of money on expensive designer clothes. What it is does mean is that you need to be appropriately dressed. Many department stores offer professional options for men and women that are both attractive and affordable.

For men, appropriate attire for a job interview includes a dark suit (in colors such as grey, black, or navy), a fitted dress shirt (that is, button-down with a collar), a conservative tie, and dress shoes. The shirt should be tucked into the pants, with a belt matching the color of the shoes (generally brown or black). Also, it is recommended that men be clean-shaven and have their hair neatly combed and styled.

For women, appropriate attire for a job interview includes a solid pant or skirt suit (in a neutral color), a coordinated blouse (preferably with a high neckline), moderate shoes (make sure they are closed-toed flats or have a low heel), and tasteful makeup and jewelry. Women's clothing should be form fitting, but not too tight or see-through.

All prospective candidates should avoid habits that may reflect poorly on them, such as chewing gum or wearing hats (unless they are worn for religious reasons), during the interview. They should also ensure that any tattoos are covered and any body piercings are either covered or the jewelry removed.

If you are ever unsure of whether an article of clothing is appropriate or not, it is always best to err on the side of conservatism. Kim Zoller, who runs a staffing agency, says that she's encountered many candidates with "great résumés, but they weren't getting the jobs because they didn't know how to dress." Don't be another promising candidate who gets turned away because of improper dress! Especially for a job as a teacher, it is important to show good judgment and that you can set a tasteful example for students that won't distract from your role as an educator.

Handling Interview Day Like a Pro

On the day of your interview, arrive ten to fifteen minutes early and make sure that your cellphone is

Confidence is key. Greet your interviewer with direct eye contact and a firm handshake.

turned off or on silent. (Even a phone on vibrate may distract you or be noticeable during an interview.) Be sure to bring a couple of extra copies of your résumé and portfolio, even if you have already submitted them by email or fax. Doing so will help you come across as prepared and ready to engage. When your interviewer greets you, make eye contact and give him or her a firm handshake.

While there is no way to know exactly what questions an employer is going to ask in an interview, there are still ways that a job candidate can prepare. First, you should do your research and be educated about the school for which you're interviewing. Information about the school can easily be obtained by visiting its website. It's a wise idea to be knowledgeable about the school's mission statement, teaching philosophy, academic programs, extracurricular activities, and whether it has any religious affiliation. It is also a good idea to learn about the school district. Be able to speak to how you will contribute to the school and the community that it serves. If you are not a member of the community—for example, you just moved to the area or are planning to commute from another city—show that you are willing to integrate and quickly adapt to the culture of the institution.

According to the National Education Association, many school districts standardize their interview questions and the topics that they will cover during an interview. Some common examples of the latter include an individual's particular style of teaching, differentiated instruction, lesson planning, technology in the classroom, emotional intelligence, and classroom management. Be ready to discuss these topics at length. Answer questions truthfully and thoughtfully.

SPOTLIGHT ON TEACHERS WHO INSPIRE: JAIME ESCALANTE

Jaime Escalante (1930–2010) was known for teaching calculus and advanced math to students at Garfield High School, located in East Los Angeles, California. Escalante revolutionized teaching by allowing those students who wanted to enroll in challenging classes to simply do so without fulfilling prerequisites. This was, for the most part, unheard of. Other teachers had previously required students who wanted to enroll in challenging classes to first pass difficult tests.

A March 2010 *NPR* article written upon Escalante's death quoted the famous educator as having shared in an interview years earlier, "You have to love the kids and make them see that they have a chance, [an] opportunity in this country to become whatever they want to." Escalante's contributions to education inspired the 1988 film *Stand and Deliver*. His work influenced other educators not to mandate prerequisites, thereby encouraging students to reach their full potential.

Being Prepared to Talk About Yourself

You may also be asked to answer more general questions such as, "What is your greatest strength?" or "What is your greatest weakness?" These and similar questions can seem intimidating at first. But they will be much easier to answer if you prepare ahead of time. When discussing your greatest strength, pick two or three skills that you possess. These skills can be knowledge-based skills (derived from education or experience—e.g., computer skills, languages, degrees, training and technical ability); they can be social skills (communication and people skills, analytical problem solving and planning skills); or they can be personal traits unique to you (dependability, flexibility, friendliness, strong work ethic, expressiveness, formality, punctuality, or being a team player). Keep in mind that your strengths should relate back to the teaching position for which you're applying, underscoring your value to the school. When discussing your greatest strengths, do so confidently but not arrogantly. Make sure to give specific examples to back up your answers, but do not spend too much time singing your own praises.

The key to discussing your greatest weakness is turning a negative trait into a positive one. You want to sell yourself. So instead of saying something such as, "I have bad organizational skills," it would be better to say something such as, "There are so many engaging activities and lessons I like to plan for my students, but class time is limited, so it is not always easy to complete all the tasks that I have planned for them. Over time, I have learned to prioritize lessons and realized that I cannot do everything that I would like to." The second response to the question shows that you are aware of the weakness but can handle it within the context of the job. You will be more likely to get the job if you respond to the question by turning your weaknesses into strengths.

If possible, have a friend help stage a mock interview with you beforehand. Give your friend a

Being cordial and friendly will help leave a positive impression on any interviewer.

list of questions that an employer might ask and answer them as though you were in a real interview. Practicing your responses will make you more confident and less likely to be nervous during the actual interview process. If you get stumped on a question during the actual interview, don't worry. All is not lost! Whatever you do, don't dismiss the question by simply saying, "I don't know." Ask questions. Perhaps you didn't understand the question. Ask your interviewer to clarify. Or begin telling your interviewer what you do know. Sometimes, speaking aloud can help you start the process of figuring out what it is you want to say.

TOP TIPS FOR INTERVIEW SUCCESS

To recap, here are some quick tips for interview success:

1. Plan to arrive early for the interview.
2. Dress for success.
3. Bring extra copies of your résumé.
4. Greet everyone you meet with a smile.
5. Gather work samples.
6. Develop and polish stories that demonstrate excellence.
7. Follow up the interview with thank-you note.

Finally, ask your own questions. It is best to think of a few beforehand. Since you have already researched the school where you are applying, this part should be easy. Asking questions of your own will show that you've done your homework and that you're genuinely interested in the position. However, it is recommended to avoid asking questions about pay before the employer offers you the job; doing so may come across as presumptuous.

At the End of the Interview

When your interview concludes, shake the employer's hands, thank the person for his or her time, and ask for a business card. Having a prospective employer's business card will enable you to spell his or her name correctly and ensure that you have the correct mailing address or e-mail address when sending a thank-you note.

A thank-you note should be short and clearly written. In the first paragraph, thank the employer for conducting the interview and express your interest in the position. In the second paragraph, briefly reiterate your skills that most impressed the interviewer (without repeating the information on your résumé word-for-word), and directly relate how these skills would be applicable to the position for which you're applying. Finally, in the third paragraph, provide the best ways to get in touch with you, including telephone number (with area code) and e-mail address. Sign the note with your first and last names. Before sending the note, proofread to check for spelling or grammatical errors. This note can be mailed or sent via email.

Sending a thank-you note will leave a good impression. Even if the school chooses not to hire you at that time, they may remember you the next time they have a vacancy to fill and contact you again.

What to Do If You Land the Job

Being offered a teaching job is a major accomplishment and something you should be proud of. Before you begin celebrating, however, you will want to confirm the details of the job offer. Keep in mind that a job offer doesn't mean that you must accept the job. Instead, after you are offered the job, you can begin negotiating the terms of employment. You can discuss such things as salary, working hours, and

Employment Contract

§ 14 Amendments and Ancillary Agreements

Before any job candidate begins celebrating an official job offer, he or she should carefully review the terms and conditions of the contract and be sure the offer is fair.

whether your employer offers health insurance or other benefits. Salary shouldn't be the focal point of your negotiation, but if you do opt to discuss it, remember to keep your request within reason. Suggest a modest market rate figure, as anything more outlandish will not be well received. When you decide to sign your contract, read it over carefully, ensuring that it includes the agreed-upon terms that you and your employer discussed. Once a contract is signed, you can begin to celebrate!

How to Handle Rejection

Unfortunately, rejection is an inevitable part of the job-hunting process. It is something that everyone— no matter how successful—has experienced at some point in his or her life. If you receive a rejection letter, try to analyze how you could improve your performance the next time around. Did you lack confidence during the interview? Do you need to review and improve your résumé? Asking these kinds of questions may not sound like much fun, but coming up with answers to them will make you a stronger candidate in the long run. Stay focused and don't let a rejection letter deter you from your goal. Keep applying to as many jobs as possible. Your dream teaching job may be just around the corner!

What If You Decide That Teaching Is Not the Right Job for You?

If, having obtained a degree in education, you decide that a traditional job in teaching is not the right career path, it may be time to explore other career options. Kristin Ann F., a high school–certified teacher on Long Island, New York, describes how her background in education helped her land her dream job: "Being so close in age to my students actually helped me to decide that, while I wanted to pursue teaching, I didn't want to do it in the conventional space or in my very early twenties. I have always been passionate about sexual health education and when I was offered the opportunity to work for a prestigious HIV/AIDS non-profit organization in New York City working with at-risk teens, I jumped at the chance to incorporate everything I had learned while getting my master's degree in adolescent education . . . To this day, it was the best job I've ever had and I never would have been successful at it without my teaching experience." As Kristin's experience conveys, an educational background in teaching paves many different career paths. Don't be dismayed—there are always other career options available.

CHAPTER Five

The Future of Teaching

Choosing a career in teaching is a wise choice. It is a field that will experience tremendous growth in the near future, as the need for teachers is on the rise in the United States. There are 1.6 million baby boomers expected to retire by 2025, many of whom are today's teachers. Furthermore, student enrollment in elementary schools, middle schools, and high schools

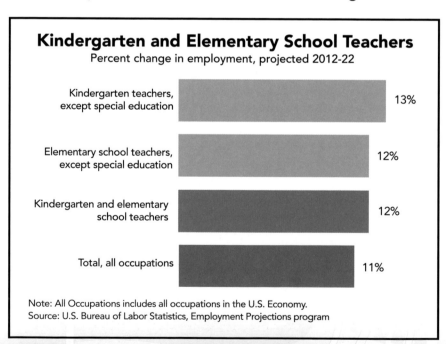

Kindergarten and Elementary School Teachers
Percent change in employment, projected 2012-22

Kindergarten teachers, except special education	13%
Elementary school teachers, except special education	12%
Kindergarten and elementary school teachers	12%
Total, all occupations	11%

Note: All Occupations includes all occupations in the U.S. Economy.
Source: U.S. Bureau of Labor Statistics, Employment Projections program

The Bureau of Labor Statistics' projected growth in employment of kindergarten and elementary school teachers in the period from 2012–2022.

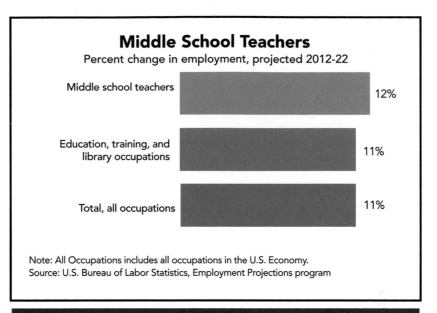

The Bureau of Labor Statistics' projected growth in employment of middle school teachers in the period from 2012–2022.

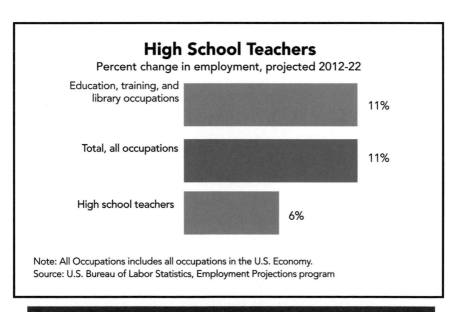

The Bureau of Labor Statistics' projected growth in employment of high school teachers in the period from 2012–2022.

is showing a steady increase. A 2007 report by the Bureau of Labor Statistics indicated that, in 2006, there were four million teaching jobs in the United States—and that number was projected to increase by 12 percent overall in the period between 2006 and 2016. This means that 479,000 new teaching positions would be created by 2016.

Government Support

After becoming U.S. president in 2009, Barack Obama and his administration began to work actively to ensure a stable future for teachers in the United States. In anticipation of the changes that would take place in the education landscape in the coming years—namely, a high number of retiring teachers coupled with an increasing need for teachers at elementary schools, middle schools, and high schools—the U.S. Department of Education released a report in September 2011 entitled "Our Future, Our Teachers: The Obama Administration's Plan for Teacher Education Reform and Improvement." The report provides valuable insights into the future of teacher education. It also explores how the United States can improve the ways in which teachers are recruited, selected, and prepared.

In the report's foreword, U.S. secretary of education Arne Duncan stressed a commitment to supporting teachers in the American education system: "Supporting a strong teaching force and school leadership is a top priority . . ." One way in which President Obama and his administration demonstrated support for teachers was the passage or revision of acts that directly—and positively—impacted teachers. One

U.S. secretary of education Arne Duncan has been one figure committed to lending government support to teachers and the education system in the United States.

such act was the American Jobs Act. When the public education sector was facing drastic budget cuts at the state and local levels during the 2008 global economic crisis, the government allocated a $30 billion fund to help prevent teacher layoffs. In 2009, the government passed the American Recovery and Reinvestment Act, which included clauses that supported college education programs in the United States by allocating funds to provide aspiring teachers with the tools and skills needed to be effective in the classroom. Namely, funding was provided to create the Race to the Top initiative—a $4.35-billion Department of Education contest to encourage innovation in teaching. Finally, the Obama administration reformed the No Child Left Behind Act in 2010.

With much-needed government support, the future of America's teachers is promising. As Duncan confirms: "We will invest needed resources in developing a teaching workforce that reflects the diversity of our students. And standards for entry into teaching will rise to a level worthy of this great profession."

TECHNOLOGY IN THE CLASSROOM

Statistically speaking, the tech wave has already hit classrooms. The following figures are proof of that:

- *Ninety-one percent of administrators say effective use of "ed tech" is critical to their mission of high student achievement.*

- *Seventy-four percent of administrators say digital content in schools increases student engagement.*

- *Seventy-seven percent of teachers say technology use in the classroom motivates students to learn.*

- *Seventy-six percent of teachers say technology allows them to respond to a variety of learning styles.*

More Technology in the Classroom

In addition to experiencing an increasing need for teachers and government legislation providing additional funding and support, the education sphere will likely undergo pedagogical changes in the years to come as well. An increased use of digital learning platforms in the classroom has already begun and will likely increase over the coming decade, which some speculate will become an enhancement to traditional face-to-face learning. Proponents of the use of digital tools in the classroom claim that technology will transform the ways in which educators teach and will help close the achievement gap, ultimately leveling the playing field by providing students from all socioeconomic backgrounds with access to open-source materials at low cost.

In its earliest manifestations, online learning has often taken the form of traditional lectures adapted to the web. In recent years, however, social and multimedia technologies have started to become more interactive and adaptive. A study funded by the U.S. Department of Education—which was cited in the *New York Times'* Bits blog in August 2009—found that on the whole, online learning produced better outcomes than face-to-face learning. According to the study's findings, "On average, students in online learning conditions performed better than those receiving face-to-face instruction." Barbara Means, the study's lead author and an educational psychologist at SRI International elaborates, "The study's major significance lies in demonstrating that online learning today is not just better than nothing—it actually tends to be better than conventional instruction." The authors of the study

Proponents of technology in the classroom claim that digital tools will revolutionize the ways that instructors teach and students learn.

concluded that students who completed all or most of their coursework online tested on average in the fifty-ninth percentile, whereas students who received only live classroom instruction scored in the fiftieth percentile.

Critics of the study are quick to point out that the authors did not gather data from enough grade K–12 sources. As the study's researchers observed, "various online learning implementation practices may have differing effectiveness for K–12 learners than they do for older students." Indeed, younger students are less likely to be equipped with the mental tools necessary to continue learning independently and may benefit from face-to-face learning and teacher interaction more than older students.

In spite of these unknowns, many ed tech investors and entrepreneurs are in favor of promoting more technology in the classroom. Venture capitalists at events such as the Arizona State University/Global Silicon Valley Summit and the Innovation Summit have strongly encouraged investment in technology-based educational products and services. Their endorsements seem well founded, as the ed tech market garnered an impressive $650 million in capital investment in 2013 alone.

While increased use of technology in the classroom may be inevitable, this does not mean that digital learning tools will replace—or become more important than—live instruction from teachers in the classroom. Rather, as the use of online educational methods expands in the coming years, teachers will play a necessary role in helping to distill students' knowledge and assist them in developing critical thinking skills about the information that they are absorbing. Online educational products can therefore be seen as tools that can be used to enhance a teacher's effectiveness in the classroom but not serve as a replacement for the teacher. Knowing how to best utilize these tools in order to maximize the effectiveness of your teaching will be of crucial importance.

SPOTLIGHT ON TEACHERS WHO INSPIRE: ANNE SULLIVAN

Anne Sullivan (1866–1936) famously taught Helen Keller how to communicate and read braille. At the young age of twenty-one, Sullivan began instructing Keller, who was deaf, mute, and blind.

Sullivan was no stranger to blindness. At the age of five, while living in severely impoverished

Anne Sullivan successfully taught her deaf and blind pupil, Helen Keller, how to communicate. The two of them are pictured here together.

conditions with her family in Massachusetts, she contracted an eye disease called trachoma, which adversely affected her sight. A few years later, at the age of eight, her mother passed away, and Sullivan was abandoned by her father and consequently sent to live at Tewksbury Almshouse, a home for the poor. It was here where she first learned about schools for the blind and became determined to escape her poverty by receiving an education.

In 1880, Sullivan enrolled in the Perkins School for the Blind. She excelled academically and was valedictorian of her graduating class. After graduating, she was recommended for a job by the school's director: he had recently learned that the Keller household in Alabama was seeking a governess for their daughter, Helen, and thought that Sullivan would be a perfect fit. Sure enough, she was.

Sullivan modeled her own teaching methods on methods that had been successfully used on a deaf and blind student whom she had known at Perkins. It was only a matter of months before Sullivan taught Keller approximately six hundred words, most of the multiplication tables, and how to read braille. Both women's successes were praised, and Keller became something of a celebrity, meeting the likes of Thomas Edison, Alexander Graham Bell, and Mark Twain.

In addition to providing private instruction, Sullivan also enrolled Keller in the Perkins School, which Keller attended sporadically. In 1900, Sullivan helped Keller continue her studies at Radcliffe College. As a result of Sullivan's efforts and Keller's hard work, Keller became the first deaf person to ever graduate from college.

(continued on the next page)

(continued from the previous page)

The two forged a bond so strong that they ended up living with each other for their rest of their lives. When Sullivan passed away in 1936, the bishop who spoke at her funeral characterized her thus: "Among the great teachers of all time she occupies a commanding and conspicuous place . . . The touch of her hand did more than illuminate the pathway of a clouded mind; it literally emancipated a soul." Indeed, Sullivan's success as an educator has had resonating effects. Her work continues to remind us of the tremendous impact that a good teacher can have on a student's life.

Adapting Your Teaching Methods

As online tools become more and more popular among educators, teachers may have to adapt their teaching methods. In 2014, Digedu, a Chicago-based retailer of digital education products that works with forty-two K–12 schools in twelve states, conducted a survey of over six hundred teachers. The results showed that a majority of teachers are excited about incorporating online learning tools into their curriculum. Nevertheless, the survey revealed that 50 percent of the teachers polled felt that they were not properly trained in technology.

Oftentimes, school districts simply lack the funds required for technology training. Many schools also lack the necessary hardware and infrastructure. In 2010, the Federal Communications Commission

As the presence of online tools becomes more prevalent in the classroom, instructors should be prepared to adjust their teaching methods accordingly.

released a survey confirming the latter, stating that half of the schools in the United States have "lower speed Internet connectivity than the average American home." While many school districts do not have the funds to make their students as technologically savvy as some educators—and companies—might prefer, this may all change in time. As a teacher, it is important to be aware of these shifts on the horizon and to be open to making changes in your curriculum in order to accommodate them.

By this point, you will hopefully have gained not only a thorough understanding of the technical aspects of the job but also an in-depth understanding of the ways in which teachers act as integral members of their communities. As conduits of knowledge, teachers equip students with the skills they will need to traipse through the world and become productive citizens. Theirs is a career path that has a profound effect on society-at-large, changing communities for the better. An educated community is an empowered one. Needless to say, the many positive effects of teaching manifest not only externally, in the positive ways in which teachers impact their communities, but also internally: teaching is a deeply fulfilling and rewarding experience.

ACCOLADE Award or honor given in recognition of a merit.

ADAPTIVE Able to adjust to different conditions, environment, responses, etc.

APPRENTICESHIP An opportunity to learn a trade through practical experience with a skilled worker in that trade.

BABY BOOMER An American born during the period between 1946 and 1965, when there was a marked increase in birthrate.

CAPITAL INVESTMENT The amount of funds invested in an enterprise.

DIGITAL LEARNING PLATFORM Online educational tool.

DIVERSITY The state or fact of being different.

FEDERAL AID Financial assistance given by the federal government.

GRANT A gift of money given for a specific purpose that does not need to be paid back.

INTEGRAL Necessary to the completeness of a whole.

INTERACTIVE When referring to a computer program or system, responding with a human user, often in a conversational way, to obtain data or commands and to give immediate results or updated information.

INTEREST RATE The percentage of a sum borrowed that must be paid back in addition to the initial sum.

LOAN Money that is given and must be repaid with interest.

NUANCED Having a subtle or slight difference or distinction in expression, meaning, response, etc.

OPEN-SOURCE Refers to computer software whose source code is available free of charge to the public to use, copy, modify, sublicense, or distribute.

PEDAGOGICAL Pertaining to pedagogy, which is the study of teaching or of instructional methods.

PROACTIVE Anticipatory or acting in preparation of future developments.

SOCIOECONOMIC Refers to the combination or interaction of social and economic factors.

SUBSIDIZED LOAN A loan that the federal government pays the interest on during periods of authorized deferment.

UNSUBSIDIZED LOAN A loan that the borrower pays the interest on during periods of authorized deferment.

America Reads
UC Santa Barbara
University Center 2523
Santa Barbara, CA 93106
(805) 893-4296
Website: http://americareads.as.ucsb.edu
The America Reads Challenge was started in 1996 by
    President Bill Clinton's administration, with the aim of
    improving national literacy.

Canadian Organization for Development Through Edu-
    cation
321 Chapel Street
Ottawa, ON K1N 7Z2
Canada
(800) 661-2633
Website: http://www.codecan.org
The Canadian Organization for Development Through
    Education supports learning by forming partnerships
    that provide resources for education.

Canadian Teachers' Federation
2490 Don Reid Drive
Ottawa, ON K1H 1E1
Canada
(866) 283-1505
Website: http://www.ctf-fce.ca
The Canadian Teachers' Federation represents
    approximately two hundred thousand elementary
    and secondary school teachers across Canada. The
    CTF promotes teachers' interests by liaising with
    federal departments and organizations whose work
    affects education, children, and youth.

Citizen Schools
308 Congress Street, 5th Floor
Boston, MA 02210
(617) 695-2300, ext. 1112
Website: http://www.citizenschools.org
Citizen Schools is dedicated to improving the quality
of education in middle schools in low-income
communities.

EnCorps Teachers Program
c/o Sherry Lansing Foundation
2121 Avenue of the Stars, Suite 2020
Los Angeles, CA 90067
(877) 619-3482
Website: http://encorpsteachers.org
The EnCorps Teachers Program recruits teachers and
tutors with backgrounds in science, technology, engineering, and math (STEM) to work with children in
disadvantaged communities.

National Education Association (NEA)
1201 16th Street NW
Washington, DC 20036
(202) 833-4000
Website: http://www.nea.org/home/49809.htm
The NEA state affiliates job board posts educational
job openings. Through its website, state-specific
teaching jobs available in a specific area can quickly
be found.

Teach for America
315 West 36th Street, 7th Floor

New York, NY 10018
(212) 279-2080
Website: http://www.teachforamerica.org
Teach for America promotes and coordinates teaching
opportunities in under-resourced public schools.

Websites

Because of the changing nature of Internet links, Rosen
Publishing has developed an online list of websites
related to the subject of this book. This site is updated
regularly. Please use this link to access this list:

http://www.rosenlinks.com/CIYC/Teach

Adams, Marilee. *Teaching That Changes Lives: 12 Mindset Tools for Igniting the Love of Learning*. Oakland, CA: Berrett-Koehler Publishers, 2012.

Ambrose, Susan, and Michael W. Bridges. *How Learning Works: Seven Research-Based Principles for Smart Teaching*. San Francisco, CA: Jossey-Bass, 2010.

Boles, Cristine. *The Flipped Classroom: Introduction to Technology and Teaching Techniques*. Missoula, MT: Phyllis J. Washington College of Education and Human Sciences at the University of Montana, 2014.

Burgess, Dave. *Teach Like a Pirate: Increase Student Engagement, Boost Your Creativity, and Transform Your Life as an Educator*. San Diego, CA: Dave Burgess Consulting, Inc., 2012.

David, Deborah Schoeberlein. *Mindful Teaching and Teaching Mindfulness: A Guide for Anyone Who Teaches Anything*. New York, NY: Simon and Schuster Digital Sales Inc., 2009.

Delpit, Lisa. "Skills and Other Dilemmas of a Black Educator." *Harvard Educational Review*, Winter 1986, pp. 379–386.

Fay, Jim, and David Funk. *Teaching with Love & Logic: Taking Control of the Classroom*. Golden, CO: Love and Logic Press, 2007.

Friere, Paul, and Myra Bergman Ramos. *Pedagogy of the Oppressed*. New York, NY: Penguin Books, 1996.

Gordon, Lynn Melby. *How to Write a Lesson Plan: Introduction to Basic Lesson Design and the 8 Keys to Good Planning*. Woodland Hills, CA: Bookmark Academic Press, 2013.

Green, Elizabeth. *Building a Better Teacher: How Teaching Works (and How to Teach It to Everyone)*. New York, NY: W.W. Norton & Company, 2014.

Hendricks, Howard. *Teaching to Change Lives: Seven Proven Ways to Make Your Teaching Come Alive*. Colorado Spring, CO: Multnomah Books, 2003.

Jensen, Eric. *Teaching with Poverty in Mind: What Being Poor Does to Kids' Brains and What Schools Can Do About It*. Washington, DC: Association for Supervision & Curriculum Development, 2009.

Johnson, LouAnne. *Teaching Outside the Box: How to Grab Your Students by Their Brains*. San Francisco, CA: Jossey-Bass, 2011.

Lemov, Doug. T*each Like a Champion: 49 Techniques That Put Students on the Path to College (K–12)*. San Francisco, CA: Jossey-Bass, 2010.

Marzano, Robert J. *The Art and Science of Teaching: A Comprehensive Framework for Effective Instruction*. Washington, DC: Association for Supervision & Curriculum Development, 2007.

Mills, Michael. *Effective Classroom Management: An Interactive Textbook*. Amazon Digital Services, Inc.

Moomaw, Sally. *Teaching STEM in the Early Years: Activities for Integrating Science, Technology, Engineering, and Mathematics*. St. Paul, MN: Redleaf Press, 2013.

Postman, Neil, and Charles Weingartner. *Teaching as a Subversive Activity*. Peaslake, Surrey, England: Delta Publishing, 1971.

Thompson, Julia G. *The First-Year Teacher's Survival Guide: Ready-to-Use Strategies, Tools & Activities for Meeting the Challenges of Each School Day*. San Francisco, CA: Jossey-Bass, 2013.

Wong, Rosemary, and Harry Wong. *The First Days of School: How to Be an Effective Teacher.* Mountain View, CA: Harry K. Wong Publications, 2004.

BIBLIOGRAPHY

Bridgestock, Laura. "How Innovation and the Reimagined Classroom Will Change Learning." Wharton University of Pennsylvania, June 12, 2014. Retrieved August 5, 2015 (http://www.topuniversities.com/student-info/university-news/thoughts-future-teaching-learning-higher-education).

Bureau of Labor Statistics. "Teachers." United States Department of Labor, January 8, 2014. Retrieved September 6, 2014 (http://www.bls.gov).

Career in Teaching. "Typical Teaching Interview Questions." November 27, 2013. Retrieved October 15, 2014 (http://www.careerinteaching.org).

Delpit, Lisa. *Other People's Children: Cultural Conflict in the Classroom.* New York, NY: New Press, 2006.

Drummond, Steve. "The Secret Lives of Teachers." NPR, October 18, 2014. Retrieved October 25, 2014 (http://www.npr.org).

Duncan, Arne. "Our Future, Our Teachers." U.S. Department of Education, September 2011. Retrieved October 12, 2014 (http://www.ed.gov).

Glass, Ira. "Is This Working?" *This American Life*, October 17, 2014. Retrieved October 17, 2014 (http://www.thisamericanlife.org).

Goldstein, Dana. "An Interview with Lisa Delpit on Educating 'Other People's Children.'" *The Nation*, March 19, 2012. Retrieved September 1, 2014 (http://www.thenation.com).

Hart, Kevin. "Six Steps to Landing Your First Teaching Job." National Education Association, 2010. Retrieved October 15, 2014 (http://www.nea.org/home/38317.htm).

Haugen, Lee. "Writing a Teaching Philosophy Statement." Iowa State University, March 1998. Retrieved October 4, 2014 (http://www.celt.iastate .edu/teaching-resources/document-your-teaching /teaching-philosophy).

Hess, Anna. "Get Schooled: 11 American Teachers Who Rocked History: Anne Sullivan." TakePart, September 4, 2013. Retrieved August 31, 2014 (http://www.takepart.com/photos/famous-teachers-american/anne-sullivan).

Hess, Anna. "Get Schooled: 11 American Teachers Who Rocked History: Emma Willard." TakePart, September 4, 2013. Retrieved August 31, 2014 (http://www.takepart.com/photos/famous-teachers -american/emma-willard).

Hess, Anna. "Get Schooled: 11 American Teachers Who Rocked History: Jaime Escalante." TakePart, September 4, 2013. Retrieved August 31, 2014 (http://www.takepart.com/photos/famous-teachers-american/jaime-escalante).

Hess, Anna. "Get Schooled: 11 American Teachers Who Rocked History: Lisa Delpit." TakePart, September 4, 2013. Retrieved August 31, 2014 (http://www .takepart.com/photos/famous-teachers-american /lisa-delpit).

Lohr, Steve. "Study Finds That Online Education Beats the Classroom." *New York Times*, Bits blog, August 19, 2009. Retrieved October 2, 2014 (http://bits. blogs.nytimes.com).

Meader, Derrick. "The Top 5 Reasons You Should Become a Teacher." About Education. Retrieved October 31, 2014 (http://teaching.about.com/od /Information-for-Aspiring-Teachers).

Sanchez, Claudio. "Jaime Escalante's Legacy: Teaching Hope." NPR, March 31, 2010. Retrieved October 15, 2014 (http://www.npr.org).

Sinberg, Laura. "Dress for Interview Success." *Forbes*, February 16, 2010. Retrieved September 3, 2014 (http://www.forbes.com).

Teach.org. "Why Teach?" Retrieved October 15, 2014 (https://www.teach.org).

Willen, Liz. "Where Will Teachers Be in the Classroom of the Future?" *The Hechinger Report*, April 21, 2014. Retrieved September 29, 2014 (http://hechingerreport.org/content/will-teachers -classroom-future_15639).

About the Author

Sophia Natasha Sunseri is a doctoral student at the City University of New York's Graduate Center, where she studies eighteenth-century British literature. She currently resides in Brooklyn, New York.

Photo Credits

Designer: Nicole Russo